Travis Wayne Goodsell
Ancient Egyptian Sign List
I.   Creation Deities

Travis Wayne Goodsell

5 January 2020

Introduction

Sir Alan Gardiner's Sign List is the most popular Ancient Egyptian Sign List as his classification is the one dominantly used. Gardiner's Sign List however, is incomplete as Sir Wallace Budge's Sign List contains extra Signs. For example, Gardiner's Deity Sign List is composed of only 11 Signs whereas Budge's Deity Sign List contains 75 Signs.

It was when I deciphered the Egyptian Pictureglyphs that I recognized the Pictureglyphs contained Signs not listed in either Sign List and therefore, were not getting translated with the Hieroglyphic or Hieratic texts. So, there needs to be an updated and complete Sign List and an updated Ancient Egyptian Grammar to include translation of Pictureglyphs.

I'm a bit disappointed that after centuries, Egyptologists still do not know the translations for the names of several of the Deities. Accordingly, I also provide the translations of the unknown meanings.

It is my intention to publish as I go along and when completed combine the category publications into one full redesigned Sign List.

Ennead Name List

Nun
Naunet
Atum
Shu
Tefnut
Geb
Nut
Osiris
Isis aka Aset
Set
Nephthys
Horus

Nun and Naunet

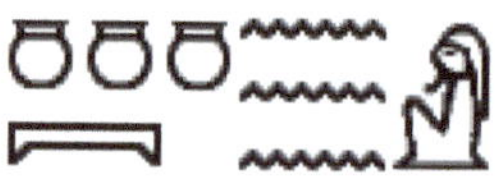

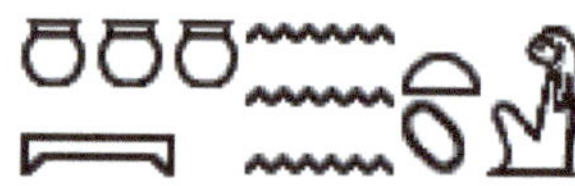

Nun   Naunet

"Inactive Waters of Space"

Atum

"To Complete or Finish"

Shu

"Air"

Tefnut

"Moisture"

Geb

"Earth/Land/Soil"

Nut

"Dark Sky"

Osiris

"The Great King and High Priest"

"The Great Seer"

Isis aka Aset

"Wife of the King"

"Mother of the Birthright Blessing Heir"

Set or Seth

"The Usurper Beast which gives birth to the Counter-Usurping Heir"

Nephthys

"Wife and Mother of the Temple Enclosure"

Horus

"The Falcon-Hawk God"

Other Associated Deities Name List

Peter aka Eyes of Horus
Anubis aka Anpu
Thoth
Ma'at

Peter aka Eyes of Horus

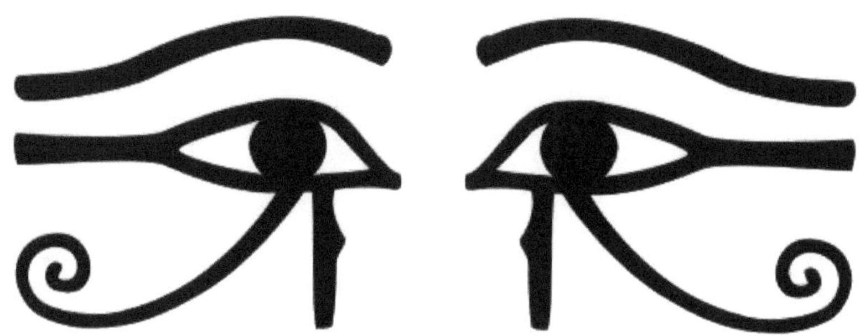

"The Great Seer"

Right Eye	Left Eye
Ra	Thoth
Sun	Moon
King	High Priest
Throne	Temple
Government	Religion

Anubis aka Anpu

"Royal Child of the Deceased"

Thoth

"He who unites the two Children or Contending Heirs"

Ma'at

"Truth, Justice, Harmony, Order"

Ogdoad (8) Name List

Nun
Naunet
Hehu
Hehut
Kekui
Kekuit
Qerh aka Amun
Qerhet aka Amunet

Nun and Naunet

Nun   Naunet

"Inactive Waters of Space"

Hehu and Hehut

Hehu   Hehut

"infinite expanse"

Kekui and Kekuit

Kekui   Kekuit

"Primordial Darkness"

Qerh aka Amun and Qerhet aka Amunet

Qerh/Amun   Qerhet/Amunet

"The Invisible Unknown"